UP AND DOWN THE MOUNTAIN

Offering The Healing Ministry
Of Christ In The Church Today

BY DONALD W. DOTTERER

C.S.S Publishing Co., Inc.
Lima, Ohio

UP AND DOWN THE MOUNTAIN

Copyright © 1992 by
The C.S.S. Publishing Company, Inc.
Lima, Ohio
Second Printing 1992

If you are the original purchaser, you may copy "A Worship Service" on pages 69-72 of this book. All other rights reserved. No other part of this publication may be reproduced, stored in a retrieval system, or transmitted in any form or by any means, electronic, mechanical, photocopying, recording, or otherwise, without the prior permission of the publisher. Inquiries should be addressed to: The C.S.S. Publishing Company, Inc., 628 South Main Street, Lima, Ohio 45804.

Scripture quotations are from the *Revised Standard Version of the Bible*, copyrighted 1946, 1952 (c), 1971, 1973, by the Division of Christian Education of the National Council of the Churches of Christ in the USA. Used by permission.

Library of Congress Cataloging-in-Publication Data

Dotterer, Donald William.
   Up and down the mountain : a healing ministry / by Donald W. Dotterer.
   p.   cm.
   Includes bibliographical references.
   ISBN 1-55673-391-7
   1. Spiritual healing—Sermons.   2. United Methodist Church (U.S.)—Sermons.   3. Methodist Church—Sermons.   4. Sermons, American.
I. Title.
BT732.5.D67
234'.13—dc20   91-25039
                                                                  CIP

9209 / ISBN 1-55673-391-7   PRINTED IN U.S.A.

To my wife Pamela,
who brings healing to my life

Table Of Contents

Preface	7
Foreword	9
Up And Down The Mountain	11
Healing And Forgiveness	17
Let Christ Speak The Word	25
To Touch The Untouchable	33
For Those On The Outside	41
Who Is This? For Palm Sunday	49
A Joyful New Beginning For Easter Sunday	55
Beginning A Healing Ministry	63
A Worship Service	69
Suggested Hymns	73
Selected Bibliography	75

Preface

This book is the product of my efforts to initiate a ministry of prayer and healing in a small, ordinary United Methodist church. My interest in the healing ministry began when I began to sense that something was missing in my ministry to sick and unhappy people.

I was intrigued by the growth and vitality of another church in our area which lies across the Youghiogheny River in McKeesport, an economically depressed community which is still struggling to overcome the disruption of its basic steel industry a decade ago. I was impressed by the comment of the church's pastor, James Laughery, who said at a meeting of ministers, that when he was asked why things were going so well in Port Vue United Methodist Church, he had to answer that the reason for the church's growth and vitality was its ministry of prayer and healing.

I attended an annual conference on healing and wholeness at Port Vue in 1989, and became interested in the theology of healing which was presented. This seminar gave me a new appreciation for the healing ministry of Jesus. It also cleared up some misunderstandings about this ministry, such as that all Christian healings are instantaneous, or that medicine does not play an important role in spiritual healing. I was also moved by the testimonies of healing which were given by people who had been in serious accidents or who had been afflicted with life-threatening diseases. Each had a powerful story to tell of how Christ had healed him in one way or another.

With the consent of my congregation, I decided that I would initiate monthly services of prayer and healing. As a means of preparing the congregation for this new ministry, I preached a series of seven sermons on the healing ministry of Jesus during the Lenten season. This book represents the fruits of that effort. The chapter on "Beginning a Healing Ministry" was written upon the suggestion of my editor, Fred Steiner. I am grateful to him for that suggestion, which I think makes the book a more useful tool for pastors wishing to initiate a ministry of healing in their churches.

Many persons have inspired me in the preparation of the manuscript. I am grateful to Jim Laughery for planting the idea of a healing ministry in my spirit, and to the people of the Christy Park United Methodist Church who have made the services of prayer and healing an important part of the life of that parish. I am especially grateful to Miss Janet Gessner, Music Director at Christy Park, for her assistance in developing these services. Most of all, I am thankful to my wife Pamela, who encouraged me to consider this new and different emphasis in my ministry.

My prayer is that Christ will continue to work through me to bring healing and wholeness to others. "Beloved, I pray that all may go well with you and that you may be in health. I know that all is well with your soul (3 John, v. 2)."

Foreword

It is Sunday noon and all across the time zone people are emerging from the dimness of churches to bright sunlight. They have sung hymns, prayed, given offerings and heard sermons. In many instances they have also celebrated the sacrament of holy communion. Which of these elements of worship is regarded as most important? In most Protestant churches it is obvious that the sermon is preeminent. The outdoor bulletin board and printed order highlight the preacher's topic. Affluent churches even print each sermon for next Sunday's distribution. In the diction of many Christians, the customary name for a minister is simply "preacher."

What is special about Christian preaching? Considered objectively, it is just a kind of rhetoric. A sermon can resemble either a didactic lecture, a political oration, a dramatic monologue, or an extended radio commercial. Unfortunately, many sermons, as preached, closely resemble these rhetorical forms not only in style but in content. While various elements of speaking contribute to the intelligibility and persuasiveness of preaching, it is the content which distinguishes it from other kinds of oral discourse.

In Christian teaching, doctrine and faith there is a bold name given to the content of preaching. It is the "Word of God." Can this traditional belief still be taken seriously? Last Sunday's sermon was not very interesting: the preacher cited the biblical text, departed from it, told some anecdotes about Christian heroes and quoted a familiar poem. Was that preaching? Was that the Word of God?

All preaching obviously cannot be the Word of God. Insofar as the sermon conveys verbally, audibly and intelligently the message of God's effective presence to us in the person and work of Jesus Christ, we may dare to say that it is a proclamation of the Word of God. Just as surely as God's eternal Word has become human and personal in Jesus Christ, and just as the Word is contained in the written words of Scripture, so the same expression of God's purpose and promise may be conveyed by the human words of the faithful preacher. When the people of ancient Galilee listened to Jesus, they both heard and beheld the present Word of God. We who hear the authentic gospel in preaching today may be hearing God's Word, too.

Two activities above all others in Jesus' ministry were preeminent: preaching and healing. These were not separate actions. When he preached about repentance, forgiveness, justice and love, his words were God's agents of healing. When he brought people back to health from illness, it was in effect preaching (or the Word) made visible. Since in Christ, God has joined preaching and healing together, it is a mark of the churches' carelessness and faithlessness to put them asunder.

It is gratifying to me, therefore, to be able to introduce these healing sermons by a good friend and former student. They mark a theological and pastoral maturing in his ministry, worthy to be shared by others beyond his congregation.

> J. Robert Nelson
> Director, Institute of Religion
> Texas Medical Center
> Houston, Texas

Up And Down The Mountain
Luke 9:37-45

Let us pray: Gracious and eternal Father, as we begin this Lenten journey, we seek to focus our hearts and minds upon understanding the ways in which you work to heal us of our afflictions. Lord grant us wisdom in these moments. May the words of our mouths, the meditations of our hearts be always acceptable in thy sight, O Lord our strength and our Redeemer. Amen.

Sir Edmund Hillary is the explorer and humanitarian from New Zealand who was the first man to stand atop Mount Everest, the highest mountain on the face of the earth. In his autobiography, titled *Nothing Venture, Nothing Win,* Hillary speaks of scaling this mountain as "the ultimate in achievement; the supreme challenge for flesh and blood and spirit."[1]

I found it rather curious in this biography that Hillary did not really write very much about his personal feelings as he stood 29,028 feet high on Mount Everest, on what must have been one of the geat "mountaintop experiences" in human history.

All that Hillary says is that "It was a great moment." After hugging his companion, he took photographs for about 10 minutes. He left a crucifix in the snow for a friend. The two men then ate a mint cake, put their oxygen back on and began to worry about the time. After 15 minutes on the top, they turned back.

Now this account of one of humanity's greatest achievements seemed to me to be somewhat anticlimactic. One would think that in this moment, one would have had a mind-expanding experience, perhaps even an experience of God. What in the world could be greater than this achievement, the fulfillment of a mountain climber's greatest dream?

The explanation, I think, can be found on the final page of this inspiring book, as Hillary writes these words:

> *Each of us has to discover his own path — of that I am quite sure. Some paths will be spectacular and others peaceful and quiet — who is to say which is the most important? For me the most rewarding moments have not always been the great moments — for what can surpass a tear on your departure, joy on your return, or a trusting hand in yours?*
>
> *Most of all I am thankful for the tasks still left to do — for the adventures still lying ahead. I can see a mighty river to challenge; a hospital to build; a peaceful mountain valley with an unknown path to cross; an untouched Himalayan summit and a shattered Southern glacier — yes, there is plenty left to do.*[2]

That is it, isn't it? After one scales the mountain, after one achieves that which one has perhaps dreamed of and worked for all of his or her life, the time comes when one must come back down from the mountaintop. A man or woman must go on with everyday living. There is always another challenge ahead of us.

Our Scripture lesson for the day from the Gospel of Luke follows that great passage called the Transfiguration, that heavenly revelation by God that Jesus was the true Son of God. Jesus' face was changed as he was invested with a heavenly light and power. Our Lord dazzled his disciples as he stood in the presence of the great prophets of Israel, Moses and Elijah. The voice of God came out of the clouds and said, "This is my Son, my Chosen; listen to him!" Now that was some mountaintop experience!"

Yes, it was on this mountaintop, away from the crowds, away from the problems and pain of the world, that Jesus met God his Father face to face. It is important for us to note the context of the meeting between Jesus and his father in heaven. We are told that Jesus took the disciples Peter, John and James with him and "went up on the mountain to pray (9:28)."

It was when Jesus was praying that his face was changed, that he received the heavenly light and power which made his clothing a dazzling white. Therefore it is important to realize that it was in the experience of prayer that Jesus discovered the meaning of his mission; it was while he was at prayer that he received his divine power.

We, too, experience God's power and light in prayer. There are times when God reveals himself to individuals with great power and glory, inspiring reverence and a sense of wonder. When God appears in such a magnificent and wonderful way, the Holy Spirit inspires people to bow down in reverence before God Almighty.

This experience of what the scholar Rudolf Otto has called "the idea of the holy" inspires a deep change in the way an individual lives his or her life. It is the tremendous mystery of God's presence in which he makes himself present to his children. When a person has this direct encounter with God, he is overcome with a deep feeling of reverence, awe and fascination. The person also feels a great sense of energy all around. Those who work with the healing ministry of the church recognize that the contact point with God's healing power is the personal desire to tap into that omnipresent divine energy.

O how we treasure those quiet moments alone with God! It is in prayer that we find strength and peace, as our spirits are filled with the spirit of God. In those moments we know that God will take care of us, and that everything will be all right. Our hearts are lifted as we hand over all that troubles us to the loving God who created us in his image. If we are suffering, we sense God's spirit suffering with us in our pain. These moments on the mountain with God in prayer are absolutely necessary if we are to live happy and fulfilled lives in a world which is so full of pain and difficulty.

That is what it means to stand on the mountaintop with God. However, what our passage for the day teaches us is that we must come down from that mountaintop to live in a world which is full of sickness, pain and suffering.

So it is significant for us to consider what Jesus did when he came down from the mountaintop. Jesus encounters a great crowd. A father of a boy who is troubled with epilepsy cries to Jesus to heal his beloved only child of this cursed affliction. Jesus then is immediately confronted with the problems and challenges of the real world. He must shift gears quickly — after communing with God in peace and glory, our Lord must now deal with what the biblical writer conceived of as a demon.

There is then much more to this passage than simply the healing of a boy with epilepsy. This dramatic confrontation between Jesus and what is called an "unclean spirit" enables us to become aware of the deep and pervasive power of evil which permeates the world we live in. We find that evil, which is contrary to the will of God, in the daily struggles of our lives.

Just read the newspaper. Eighty-seven people are burned to death in a New York City fire, allegedly because one man got angry with his girlfriend. We read that a 13-year-old boy does not want to see his father who has been released from prison early on his good behavior. Why? Because his father had poured kerosene around the bed where his six-year-old son lay, and set it on fire. The boy survived, but with third-degree burns.

The reality of evil. It is there among us almost everywhere we look. Humanity's inhumanity to individuals and groups of people has a long and sordid history. Ever since Cain murdered Abel, we have experienced evil spirits working deep within the human soul as people destroy one another. We may not understand the violence which is the result of hatred and bitterness, but we feel at the very least that we can explain crimes which philosophers categorize as moral evil, that is, evil that is caused by one person's cruelty towards another human being.

But what can we say of the evil that manifests itself as undeserved illness in the lives of so many people whom we know and love? In most cases, disease cannot be categorized as moral evil, that is, evil that is caused by one person's sin towards another human being. What do we say, what do we do, when, as in our Scripture lesson today, a child is afflicted with an incurable disease? The more difficult question is, what does God think, and what does God do in the midst of such terrible and senseless suffering?

Theologians and philosophers speak of this issue as the problem of evil. It is for pastors the most difficult question that must be faced in the ministry. As a pastor, I cannot explain to you why some suffer more than others, or why some are healed of their afflictions and others are not.

I do not believe that people are punished by God for their sins by their illness; I do not think that we feel pain because God is trying to teach us some sort of painful lesson that will bring us into line. As the Bible reminds us, the rain falls upon the just and the unjust in God's world (Matthew 5:45).

What we can be sure of is that our God is a God who loves us all the time. In the end, God will be victorious over evil, and all things will work together for good. Furthermore, I believe that our God is a God who suffers with us, that God feels our pain as we feel it. This is how he strengthens us. So together, with the spirit of God in our hearts and in our souls, we can make ready to do battle with the evil which plagues our lives and thwarts God's good intentions for us in this world.

William Sloane Coffin, pastor of Riverside Church in New York City, wrote these words down upon the untimely death of his son Alex in an automobile accident:

> *Nothing so infuriates me as the incapacity of seemingly intelligent people to get it through their heads that God doesn't go around in this world with his finger on triggers, his fist around knives, his hands on steering wheels. God is dead set against all unnatural deaths. And Christ spent an inordinate amount of time delivering people from paralysis, insanity, leprosy and muteness. . . . The one thing that should never be said when someone dies is, "It is the will of God." Never do we know enough to say that. My own consolation lies in knowing that it*

> was not the will of God that Alex die; that when the waves closed over the sinking car, God's heart was the first of all our hearts to break.[3]

My friends in Christ, God is always there with us, no matter what may happen. Somehow, some way, God will help us in our greatest hours of need. Yes, Jesus healed the boy with epilepsy. His power is so great that he can heal us of our afflictions as well.

But in those instances where the healing we want is not the healing we receive, we need to remember that through our prayers, in our times on the mountaintop, we will receive the strength to confront the power of evil in this world. God is always victorious and God always suffers with us when we are in pain and despair. God may not be able to defeat all evil on earth, but in the end, in the life to come, God will heal us of every sorrow.

May our prayer this day be that we may find Christ in prayer. May we be healed of all that from which we suffer.

> *Benediction: Gracious and eternal God, we have worshiped and prayed together. We have felt the presence of your Spirit which heals us. As we go from this place, may we share that power with others.*
>
> *Now may the love of God, the peace of Christ and the fellowship of the Holy Spirit be with you always. Amen.*

---

1. Sir Edmund Hillary, *Nothing Venture, Nothing Win* (New York: Coward, McCann & Geoghegan, Inc., 1975), p. 130.

2. *Ibid*, p. 308. Quoted with permission.

3. William Sloane Coffin, "Alex's Death." In *Sermons from Riverside*, a sermon preached at Riverside Church, New York City on January 23, 1983, p. 2. Quoted by Kent D. Richmond in *Preaching to Sufferers* (Nashville: Abingdon, 1988), p. 69.

Healing And Forgiveness

Luke 5:18-26

> *Let us pray: Gracious and eternal God, we continue our worship during this season of Lent, seeking to understand the gifts of healing which you bring to our lives. Lord, in these moments, may we catch a glimpse of the truth that your spirit can touch and heal us of our afflictions. In the precious name of Jesus we pray, Amen.*

There is a story about an old Maori woman in the country of New Zealand who had earned a reputation for being an argumentative, combative person, for which she received the nickname of "Warrior Brown." She would become especially belligerent when she became drunk and angry.

However, Warrior Brown's life was changed, when by the grace of God and the love of some missionaries, she accepted Jesus Christ as her Lord and Savior. One day at an outdoor meeting, she was giving her testimony to the love of God in Christ, when someone in the crowd threw a potato at her, bruising her face. The woman quietly just picked the potato up and put it into her pocket. Then she went home. Had this incident happened before Ms. Brown's conversion to Christ, the potato hurler would have had to flee or risk life and limb.

Nothing more happened in relation to this incident until much later when the the church held its annual Harvest Festival. "Warrior Brown" had become a fine gardener, and she brought with her a sack of good potatoes. What she had done was to plant in God's good earth the insulting potato which was hurled at her in hostility, and this potato had brought an increase as it became an offering of love to Jesus Christ.[1]

The gift that Warrior Brown brought that day to the Harvest Festival was much more than a sack of potatoes. The real gift, the one that cost something, was the offering of a forgiving heart, completely absent of hatred and resentment.

In our gospel lesson for the morning, we read the dramatic story which combines an account of Jesus as healer with a pronouncement that Jesus had the authority to forgive sins. The story is set in what was probably a one-story, one-roomed house with a flat roof. Jesus' reputation as a healer of the sick was well-known by now, and a great throng of people both inside and outside of the house prevented any entry, especially for one who was seriously handicapped.

There was in this crowd a man who was paralyzed. He and his friends knew that they must get close to this Jesus in order for him to be able to be healed. The friends must have been men of great faith, and they would not be deterred from reaching the touch of the Master. Since they could not get in the door, they decided to dismantle the roof, and gain entry in this way. One lesson which this passage teaches us then is that the faith of this crippled man's friends played an important part in his healing. It says something to us about how we and our loved ones need to be persistent in faith and prayer when someone is suffering from an affliction.

Sometimes we need the combination of patience and persistence as we await healings. This is difficult for many of us, since when we hear of dramatic faith healings, most often they are of the instantaneous nature. Even though this is not characteristic of most healings, this is what we want and expect. When healings do not occur in this way, then we and our loved ones are disappointed.

Agnes Sanford uses the example of Thomas Edison's invention of the incandescent light bulb to illustrate how it is that God's healing energy comes into our lives. Edison had tried and failed hundreds of times to find the right wire to transmit electricity. When he failed, he did not say, "It is not the will of electricity to shine continuously in my wire." Instead he tried again and again. Edison believed that "it was in the will, that is, in the nature of electricity to produce this steady light." His conclusion was that he would just have to find the proper adjustment to the laws of electricity in his method. Edison tried more than 6,000 times before he was able to make electricity shine through a wire. As Sanford says, "That is faith."[2]

We are told that when Jesus saw the "faith" of the paralyzed man's friends, the first thing that he said to the crippled man was "Man, your sins are forgiven you." Now why did he say this? What was so crucial about the forgiveness of sins when a man needed to be healed of a physical handicap?

To understand this passage, we must remember that in ancient Israel, one's sin and one's suffering were usually connected. In contrast to other Near Eastern cultures, Hebrew theology held that there was only one God, the all powerful Creator and sustainer of all living things. This Yahweh was a deity who was totally in control of all human and natural events.

There is in the Old Testament, beginning with the story of Adam and Eve, a close relationship between sin and illness. It was because of Adam's sin of eating the forbidden fruit that all physical evils, including illness, entered the world. Therefore after the Fall, there developed in the Old Testament the belief that physical evil came from God who was the all omnipotent ruler of the universe.

For this reason then, disease and injury became viewed as a consequence and punishment of human sin. They are seen as clearly within the realm of God's control. In Deuteronomy 32:39 God says: "I kill and I make alive; I wound and I heal." Disease, as seen as part of God's anger against sin, was witnessed as being inflicted on both individuals and nations. Different biblical characters were stricken with leprosy when they were disobedient to God. We remember the boils that came as a plague upon the Egyptians when they refused to set the people of Israel free from slavery.

Therefore, it was because of this belief that physical afflictions were associated with human sin that Jesus found it necessary to say to this paralyzed man, "your sins are forgiven you." If Jesus had not assured this man that his sins were forgiven, then he never would have believed that he could be healed, because he had been taught by his tradition that his paralysis was the result of his wrongdoing. Jesus knew that if a person does not believe that he or she can be cured, then there can be no healing.

Furthermore, by combining the forgiveness of sin with healing, Jesus very skillfully blunted the criticism of the Scribes and Pharisees. These religious leaders were the ones who propagated the notion that if a person was ill, then he or she must have sinned. Although on one hand they objected to Jesus' offering forgiveness to this man, they witnessed this healing as a proof that the man's sins were actually forgiven.

One of the great correctives that Jesus brought to our faith tradition is the truth that people are not punished by God with illness. It is true that our sins can make us sick, as people often become emotionally upset when they act in selfish, greedy and harmful ways toward other people. But Jesus taught us that our God is a God who loves us, one who wants us to live healthy and happy lives. Our God is a God who forgives us for our trespasses. The Lord desires that we be healed.

What is more poisonous than the petty hatreds and grudges that we hold against co-workers, family members and former friends? How seldom are the concerns that so bitterly divide us of any great consequence? So often they are rooted in squabbles over the superficial issues of money, power and possessions.

A husband said to his wife, "Why do you keep talking about the mistakes which I made in the past? I thought you had forgiven me?" The wife replied, "I have forgiven you; I just wanted to make certain that you don't forget that I have forgiven you." This is not the kind of forgiveness that Jesus was talking about, for this sort of forgiveness, which keeps a file on past trespasses, will not bring healing, either to an interpersonal relationship or to a physical body. God's grace forgives us completely; we are called to do the same so that we might be set free from the encumbrances and bondage of the past.

Ernest Campbell of the Fifth Presbyterian Church in Manhattan wrote more than 25 years ago about a clergyman in

Boston who for some reason had kindled the anger of one of his female parishioners. She wrote poison pen letters and was tireless in her efforts to build up dissension against the pastor.

After this unpleasant relationship had diminished over time, the woman quite unexpectedly moved to Arizona. Many months later the minister received a letter from her saying simply that she had a change of heart and that she was enormously sorry for what she had done. Reverend Campbell telegrammed a three-word message: "Forgiven, forgotten, forever." No copy retained. When God extends the blessing of forgiveness to us, we are freed to completely let go of the past.[3]

James Wagner, in his book titled *Blessed to Be a Blessing*, asks this question: "How many people . . . look upon forgiveness as a crucial key to personal good health? Not only is forgiveness good for one's soul and one's social life, it is equally good medicine for one's mental and physical well-being.[4]

This is the connection which Jesus made in his healing of the paralytic. Furthermore, we don't need to look very far in our own lives to see that the withholding of forgiveness from others can be a source of both physical and mental anguish. Why do people get ulcers? So often it has to do with resentment and hard feelings toward other people. You have heard people say, "he's a pain in the neck," or "she gives me a headache" or he "makes me sick to my stomach." It's true! Our inability to forgive and forget truly and totally can cause both short-term and long-term illnesses.

Medical researchers are helping us to understand the relationship between forgiveness and good health. A Canadian physician by the name of Dr. Hans Selye has done extensive research in the area of stress and distress. His study is primarily in the area of biochemistry, and yet he has discovered that positive emotions and attitudes, such as forgiveness, thanksgiving, praise and joy can actually enhance and improve a person's health. Negative emotions and attitudes such as resentment, anger, revenge and jealousy have a debilitating, disease-inducing effect on the body.[5]

Dr. A. M. Master, a consulting cardiologist at Mount Sinai Hospital in New York a number of years ago told a group of heart specialists that angina patients must learn not to get angry at their wives over little things, or to worry about incidents such as getting overcharged or shortchanged. If they could simply learn this lesson they would not only stay alive, but also live longer and more happily than if they had never had a chest pain. But Dr. Masters adds, "only 25 percent of the people with angina are able to avoid emotional distress and keep calm in the face of aggravation and frustration."[6]

Legend has it that when Leonardo da Vinci was painting his famous fresco, *The Last Supper*, one of his apprentices annoyed him with a heedless remark. It made the great artist very angry. He yelled at the young man, who ran away, embarrassed and ashamed.

Da Vinci then turned back to his work, at which point he was painting the face of Jesus. But try as he might, he just couldn't get the face of the Master onto the wet plaster. However, when da Vinci had asked the forgiveness of his young apprentice, he returned to painting the fresco. His genius was restored and he painted the face of Christ without a flaw.

My friends in Christ, Jesus comes to forgive our sins. The real struggle is to allow that forgiveness to touch us in the depths of our hearts, to allow Christ to reach into our hearts and minds so that we might be set free from sins of our past and fully healed of our guilt. Furthermore, we need God's great power and love to help us to do that which is surely most difficult for us: to forgive and forget completely the ways in which others have hurt and offended us. We need to allow Christ to bring us an inner healing that will enable us to live in peace and harmony with all whom we meet.

Let our prayer this day be that we may allow God's healing power to come to us through the blessing of forgiveness. May we be healed and made new through his love.

Benediction: Gracious and eternal God, we have worshiped together, we have reflected upon how it is that you can help us to live together in peace and love. Now as we go from this place, may your richest blessings be upon us as we go out into the world to spread the good news that we are forgiven and saved and healed.

The blessing of God the Father, Son and Holy Spirit, be among you and remain with you always. Amen.

---

1. "The Beautiful Story of Warrior Brown." Lenten Meditation. 240000 Research Drive, Farmington Hills, Michigan: Parish Service Company. No author or date given.

2. Agnes Sanford, *The Healing Light* (St. Paul: Macalester Park Publishing Co., 1955), p. 25.

3. Spencer Morgan Rice, "The Robe, the Ring, and the Shoes." Sermon preached at Trinity Church in Boston, March 13, 1983, p. 3.

4. James Wagner, *Blessed to Be a Blessing* (Nashville: Upper Room Press, 1980), p. 77.

5. Hans Selye, quoted by Wagner in *Blessed,* p. 84.

6. A. M. Master, quoted by Morton T. Kelsey, in *Psychology, Medicine & Christian Healing* (San Francisco: Harper & Row, 1988), p. 220.

Let Christ Speak The Word
Luke 7:1-10

> *Let us pray: Gracious and eternal God, today we come to you seeking to deepen our understanding of the ways in which you are present and working in our lives to heal us of our afflictions. May we in these moments receive the gift of wisdom. In Jesus' name we pray, Amen.*

You may be familiar with the life story of Thomas Dooley, the Christian military doctor who devoted his life to serving sick and dying people living in Vietnam and Laos in the 1950s. When he died of cancer in 1961, the world considered his death a tragedy, which indeed it was.

One of Tom Dooley's books is titled *The Night They Burned the Mountain*. The setting is the Asian country of Laos in the hot, dry season preceding the wet and rainy monsoons. It was a period of intense fighting between the Communist and Laotian government forces who were supported by the Americans.

Late one night, as Dooley was sitting in the main room of his house, he heard a great racket outside. Sensing that something was happening out there, he took a flashlight and walked out onto the front porch.

Dr. Dooley writes that the mountains all around the village looked as though they were covered by swarms of lightning bugs — they were blinking, flickering lights in all directions. They looked almost like Japanese lanterns in a parade.

Then he saw one section of the jungle catch on fire. Then came more and more fire. Suddenly, one whole mountain slope burst into a blinding glare of yellow flame — the flickering lights he had seen were people moving with torches to set fire lights he had seen were people moving with torches to set fire to the jungle. As oppressive rolls of heat poured down the valley into the village, the young doctor felt terrified. Were these communists burning the jungle down? Was this another of their horrible atrocities?

Then one of the Laotian helpers said to the physician: "Do not fear. This is the night they burn the mountain."

Tom Dooley learned that evening that the burning of the mountain was a religious and agricultural ritual; that the village sorcerers and astrologers chose this special night for people to set fire to the slopes of the mountains. The end result would be that the ashes would cover the ground, and when the rains came in a few days, the ground would be rich and fertile. In this black, scorched earth, the tribes would plant their rice roots and from the seedlings would grow the poor mountain rice which was the staple of the villagers' diet.

As Dr. Dooley and his friend watched the mountain burn for many hours, the young doctor reflected upon what was happening. "What would become of these mountains and these tribes?" he asked himself. "What would happen to their kingdom and their freedom when the war was finally settled?"

A few days later, when the heavy monsoon rains came, Dooley writes that in this land and in this season, God was everywhere. He saw God in the mountains, in the air, in the mist, in the morning fog. He heard God in the monsoon rain tapping on the thatched roof. God's hand of life was also present in the people he served as a doctor.[1]

Now I share this story with you because I think that it speaks to us of the way in which God is revealed to the person of faith who opens his or her mind and spirit to the Lord God. It speaks of how God can be seen by one who has chosen to serve Christ, in this instance by a man who had made healing others his purpose in living. It is about seeing God through the eyes of faith by having a genuine concern for one's fellow humans.

In our Scripture lesson for the morning, we have another account of a healing by Jesus; however, the circumstances of this miracle are quite different from the others that we have been considering. This story concerns a Roman centurion who was presumably an officer in the Army of Herod Antipas. We need to understand that a centurion was a highly respected and powerful member of the armed forces. He would have had to have been an outstanding individual to have achieved this position, which was the equivalent in rank to a sergeant major in our army of today. Centurions are well thought of throughout the New Testament.

We are told that this centurion had a slave who was very dear to him. This gives a clue as to the nature of the man. According to Roman Law, slaves were considered to be merely a thing or a tool, for they had no civil rights. The master could treat a slave in any way he liked; he was free even to take the slave's life if he so desired. When a slave was past the time when he could work productively, he would be put out of the household to die. So clearly, for this army officer to love a slave was indeed unusual. This tells us that he was a man of great compassion.

You will remember the circumstances of the healing of the paralytic which we discussed last week. The friends of the handicapped man believed that their companion would not be healed unless he was touched by the hand of Jesus. Since they could not get into the house where Jesus was working because of the great crowd, they dismantled the roof so that their friend could be healed.

In today's lesson, we see a very different approach to healing. The centurion sends out some elders to ask them to bring Jesus to come and heal his beloved slave. Jesus agrees to come and sets out to the house of the centurion. The officer is described to Jesus by the Jewish elders as a good man, one who has loved the nation of Israel and built their temple. For this reason they have judged the centurion to be "worthy" of Jesus' assistance.

Then something very strange and unexpected happens. The centurion sends friends to Jesus who relay this message: "Lord, do not trouble yourself . . . . But say the word and let my servant be healed." When Jesus hears this, he is amazed. He tells the crowd which is following him that "not even in Israel" had he found such faith. When the friends of the centurion returned to the house, they found that the slave had been healed.

Now what is the message for us in this story? I think that the lesson for us is that even though Jesus may be absent in the flesh, his very word is enough to heal us. We remember in Genesis that when God began to create the world, all he did was say "Let there be light, and there was light." God had only to speak and his will was done.

So it is also with God's son Jesus, who according to the Gospel of John, was "the Word became flesh and dwelt among us, full of grace and truth . . ." The Word of God revealed in Jesus Christ has great power among us.

The theology which informs the healing ministry of the church holds that God is both transcendent and immanent. What this means is that God is not only in the heavens, but that God in Christ lives in our minds and our bodies as well. To receive and to share the power of healing, we must tap into the omnipresent power of God in Christ through prayer for ourselves and for others.

Modern science has informed us that contrary to what was believed for centuries, the universe and everything in it is not made up of irreducible bits of matter, but of energy and vibrations. The abandonment of the materialistic interpretation of how the world is constructed opens up new ways of understanding how the power of the Holy Spirit is present and working in and through everything in God's creation.

One of the more intriguing theories has been developed by a Princeton University physicist by the name of Edward Witten. He invites us "to jump into a world of infinite dimension."[2] Some have labeled his hypothesis as a "theory of everything." The "string theory," as it is commonly called, does away with the familiar image of a universe composed of billiard ball-like particles which are pushed and pulled by forces of gravity and electricity. In the 1920s, quantum physics revealed that the billiard balls had wave-like properties like vibrations. String theory holds that these string-like vibrations make up everything in the universe from lightning bugs to gravity to gold.[3]

If we conceive of the universe in this manner, then perhaps it is easier for us to grasp, at least on an intellectual level, how it is that God's healing energy is present and working everywhere at once in our world. The challenge for us as people of faith is to learn how it is that we might work in concert with the Holy Spirit so that this healing energy may enter the bodies and minds of those who suffer from mental and physical illnesses.

Agnes Sanford describes how it is that we might transmit the healing power of God to those who are afflicted: "Then if we would help man through intercession, we must hold God by one hand and man by the other hand, never separating ourselves either from the love of God or from the love of man. As we do this by the indwelling of Jesus Christ, God can work through our normal human love in ways that we do not see."[4]

So it is that the lesson which today's Scripture lesson teaches us is that God is everywhere among us. In the midst of our most difficult moments, we can call upon God in Christ to help us, yes even to heal us.

Christ need only speak to us nearly 2,000 years after he walked the earth, and his life-giving power and love will reach into our bodies and minds and souls as we are cured of all our physical and mental afflictions. What a comfort it is to know that Christ is always with us, wherever we may be, whatever we are doing. We need only call on Christ and he will give his Word so that we may receive healings. This is the great hope and promise of our faith.

The great Japanese Christian, Toyohiko Kagawa, tells how a Christian missionary helped him to understand the love of God. One time when Reverend Kagawa was spending a sick period alone during his days as a student, the missionary man knocked at the door. He requested that the man not enter. He said, "Do not come in! I have a contagious disease."

But the missionary entered anyway and said, "I have something more contagious than disease. I have come with the love of God."[5]

A number of years ago when I was living in Massachusetts, I had an opportunity to hear an address by that small and saintly woman named Mother Teresa, the Roman Catholic nun who has lived her life in service to the suffering and destitute in the streets of Calcutta, India. One is truly moved by standing in her presence.

Mother Teresa was asked on one occasion what words she lived by, and she responded by quoting another Teresa, Saint Teresa of Avila:

> *Christ has*
> *No body on earth but yours;*
> *No hands but yours;*
> *No feet but yours;*
> *Yours are the eyes*
> *Through which is to look out*
> *Christ's compassion to the world;*
> *Yours are the feet*
> *With which he is to go about*
> *Doing good;*
> *Yours are the hands*
> *With which he is to bless now.*[6]

My friends in Christ, God in Christ is indeed all about us. He need only speak the word and we may be healed. What we need to understand is that as Christians, as members of the body of Christ, we are the ones who carry the love of God to those who are in need. We are the ones who can serve as a channel of God's love as he heals those we know and love. God is everywhere, because we carry his power and spirit in our hands as the body of Christ in the world.

May our prayer this day be that we have the faith of the Roman centurion. May we carry the Word of Christ to all, so that we can be agents of Christ's healing ministry.

Benediction: Lord we have heard your word and sung praises to your name. As we go from this place, may your love and presence be with us always. The blessing of God the Father, Son and Holy Spirit, be among you and remain with you always. Amen.

---

1. Thomas A. Dooley, *The Night They Burned the Mountain* (New York: Farrar, Straus, Cudahay, 1960), p. 135.

2. Edward Witten, in K. C. Cole, "A Theory of Everything," *New York Times Magazine,* October 18, 1987, p. 21.

3. Cole, "A Theory," *Times Magazine,* October 18, 1987, p. 22.

4. Agnes Sanford, *The Healing Light* (St. Paul: Macalester Park Publishing Co., 1955), p. 147.

5. *The Preacher's Illustration Service,* Bonus Issue, 1988, p. 2.

6. St. Teresa of Avila in *A Guide to Prayer for Ministers and Other Servants,* ed. Rueben P. Job and Norman Shawchuck (Nashville: The Upper Room,, 1983), pp. 22-23.

To Touch The Untouchable
Luke 5:12-16

Let us pray: Gracious and eternal God, we pause now to hear your word as we worship together in this holy season of Lent. Today we continue to explore the powers of prayer, faith and healing which you have granted to us. In these times together O God, we pray that you would open our hearts and our minds so that we may have faith and understanding. In Jesus' name we pray, Amen.

You may have heard the expression, "He has an Atlas complex." This usually refers to an individual who seems to have an exaggerated sense of his or her own importance. Or it may refer to the person who feels that he or she is the only one who can do a certain job, make important decisions, take care of themselves or other people.

It is helpful for us to remember the Greek legend of Atlas. Atlas is the man who got himself into trouble when he went to war against Zeus, the presiding God of the Greek pantheon, the ruler of the heavens and father of other gods and mortal heroes. The great and powerful Zeus won the battle of course, in part because he was assisted by his famous 100-handed monster. The punishment which Atlas received was the job of forever holding the world on his shoulders.

The story of Atlas is, of course, a myth. However, you and I both know that there are many people who go through life holding the weight of the world on their shoulders. Furthermore, it is probably true that most of us have this problem ourselves to some extent. We feel that we must bear all of our burdens by ourselves. We believe that we stand alone when we are faced with either crisis situations or ongoing problems. This tendency often becomes more evident whenever we are confronted with a serious illness or injury.

In a town named Lourdes which is nestled in the French Pyrenees, there is a place of worship which is celebrated for miracles of healing. There is a story about a World War II veteran with an amputated leg who went one day to the shrine for prayer. As he hobbled up to the shrine, a bystander said, "Poor man. Does he think that God will give him back his leg?" The veteran heard the remark and replied: "No sir, I don't expect God to give me back my leg. I am going to pray to him to help me live without it."[1]

Too often we do not look to God first to help us find the strength to deal with life's afflictions and disappointments. Unfortunately, for many of us, prayer is considered as a last resort when we are having physical or interpersonal problems. Why is it that we do not turn in the first place to the greatest power of all to help us through the dark moments of our lives?

This is the reason why I believe that the lesson from the Gospel of Luke is so important. We have here the story of a man who came to Jesus "full of leprosy." In Palestine during the time which Jesus lived, people suffered from two different kinds of leprosy. The first kind was like a bad skin disease, while the second was the more serious, beginning as a small spot and then rotting away the flesh until only a stump of a hand or leg remained.

We know today that leprosy is not a tropical disease, as cases of leprosy have been reported all over the world. It is generally an affliction which is the result of poverty, disease and poor diet. Leprosy is not hereditary, although like many diseases among the poor and undernourished, it can be transmitted from parents to children. It is not highly contagious, and it is almost impossible for a healthy person to contract leprosy.

Lepers in Jesus' time not only suffered from the literal wasting away of their physical bodies, but they also suffered social isolation. According to the ritual laws in the Book of Leviticus, the leper was expected to separate himself and to cry out "unclean, unclean," whenever other people came near him. His illness was of the body, but it also became an affliction of the mind because of his social rejection. One authority claimed that when the wind was blowing from a leper toward a healthy person, the leper was to stand at least 50 yards away. The leper was not avoided because he was thought to be contagious, but rather because he was considered to be defiled in a religious sense (Leviticus 13-14).

This then was the condition of the man who presented himself to Jesus for healing. We need to consider very carefully what this man said as he approached the Master. We read that when he saw Jesus, he bowed to the ground and "begged" Jesus to help him saying: "Lord, if you will, you can make me clean."

What is important here for us is the fact that this man had not accepted his suffering and impending death as inevitable. He was not going to shoulder his pain and suffering all alone. No, he approached Jesus and came right out and asked the Master to heal him, for he believed without reservation that Jesus could heal him of his cursed affliction.

This man was not willing to accept the conventional wisdom and law which dictated that he isolate himself in a private world of hopelessness and despair. He was willing to take the risk of being condemned by the establishment so that he could once again find the fullness of life.

Jesus, of course, responded to this man by saying to him, "Yes, I will heal you." Jesus reached out his hand and touched the man, and in doing so Jesus touched the one who was supposed to be untouchable. It is for this reason that the man was healed.

My former teacher, Howard Clark Kee, has shown that Jesus is depicted in the gospel narratives as performing healings in such a way as to open up participation in the covenant community for those who were for legalistic reasons denied acceptance. "He healed persons who were off-limits by the standards of Jewish piety . . . ," such as tax-collectors, foreigners, lepers and even a woman with a menstrual condition.[2] His hand went out to the ones whom everyone else avoided like the plague.

There is a story about Saint Francis which may help us to understand how Jesus heals, and how we can be a conductor through which God's Holy Spirit heals others. One day Francis was riding home to Assisi. He was struggling with his call to God's work, but he was still living the life of a fashionably dressed son of an atistocrat. Suddenly he saw the sight that he was most afraid of — a person suffering from leprosy. Then a tremendous change came over Francis. Filled with a power that was not his own, Francis put money into the leper's hand, and then putting his lips to the leper's flesh, he kissed that diseased hand with his own clean lips. The leper, seeing that Francis was filled with love, held him and gave him the kiss of peace, and Francis kissed him back. Francis then climbed on his horse and rode home with joy. On that day Francis began his ministry with the lepers, visiting them and bringing them gifts. All of this happened because he overcame his fear of touching the untouchable.

Likewise, we need not be afraid to get near to people who are seriously ill. The first step is to touch with compassion the person who stands in need of prayer and healing.

Why is it that we do not come to Jesus first when we are suffering physical or emotional pain? Why is it that we do not enter into prayer immediately when we learn that we or those we love are suffering from a potentially serious illness? No doubt you have heard it said when someone is critically ill, "Well, we've done everything we can do. All we can do now is pray."

This statement reveals two discouraging truths about the depths of our faith. First of all, it suggests that prayer is a last resort. Secondly, this statement indicates a lack of trust in the power of prayer to actually bring physical healing to men, women and children.

It is in prayer that we encounter the Christ who can actually heal us. The New Testament narrative makes it very clear that the healing of the sick was one of the most important aspects of Jesus' earthly mission. For various reasons, over the centuries, the church has given little attention to this part of Christ's ministry of healing.

Nevertheless, an unbiased and fresh reading of the Bible demonstrates that Jesus showed tremendous interest in both the physical and mental well-being of the people whom he met. Nearly one-fifth of the gospel narrative is devoted to the healing ministry. Jesus' words and actions prove that for our Lord, sickness and pain were in direct opposition to God's love and his desire that people live joyful and healthy lives.

Therefore, if we take the records of the New Testament seriously, we realize that the God revealed in Jesus wants us to come directly to him in the first place, and not be afraid to ask for healing. For reasons known only unto God, it may be that the healing we pray for may not occur in the way in which we have asked for it to happen. Nevertheless, when we come to God in prayer, there is always some kind of healing. If we do not receive a physical healing, we will be strengthened and comforted by God's sustaining love. In one way or another, God's grace will touch us, even though we may feel that we are untouchable.

After making a careful and factual study of the numerous healings which have occurred at the aforementioned Shrine of Lourdes in France, John Sutherland Bonnell makes this observation: "One fact seems apparent: the Creator has so fashioned our universe that there are inherent in it certain powerful forces that work for human restoration and healing."[3] Personal and corporate prayer is that experience which enables our spirits to connect with the healing energy of God.

Furthermore, as George Buttrick has written, in those instances in which prayer does not bring a physical healing, it helps us in other ways. "Prayer's greatest healing is . . . not healing, but the courageous acceptance of the terms of mortal life. True prayer does not evade pain, but gains from it insight, patience, courage and sympathy; and at long last, makes it an oblation to God. True healing does not sidestep death, but greets it. This is healing beyond healing."[4]

Paul Brand is a British physician who has worked with lepers for most of his medical career. He is recognized throughout the world for his innovative work in restoring to functional use the crippled or paralyzed hands of lepers. His work has been done at the Christian Medical College and Hospital in Vellore, India.

Dr. Brand hadn't worked very long with the lepers there before he began to realize that the prevailing ideas about the nature of the disease called leprosy were just wrong. Perhaps his most important discovery was that since lepers could not feel pain because the disease had killed their nerve endings, they were destroying their fingers, toes and arms because they were not warned by sensations of pain when they smashed or burned their hands or feet. He began to look at the total problem of leprosy, how it affected the body and the mind. Brand asked himself how it might be combatted and healed.

Dr. Brand developed surgical techniques which restored the use of hands and eyes. He accomplished much in removing the superstition from this dreaded and misunderstood disease. As he developed various methods of reconstructive surgery, he also pursued ways in which the human beings who suffered from this disease could be helped personally and psychologically.

But as Norman Cousins has observed, there is one aspect of his work which is more important than all the others. Dr. Brand "is a doctor who, if he could, would move heaven and earth" so that these people could feel pain the way that we feel.[5] Paul Brand believed that if he could do this, then he would be restoring life to those who had been living their own death. Dr. Brand cared that much about the people whom he had been sent to heal. He was able to heal these sick and often forgotten human beings because he cared enough to give his life to touch them with his hands, his mind and his heart.

My friends in Christ, the healing power of God is real. God will come to us, Christ will touch our lives, if we come to him in faith and prayer. This season of Lent, let us open our hearts, minds and bodies to the love and power of God so that we may be healed, and that God's power may work through us so that we might play a part in the healing of others.

> *Benediction: Our Lord and our God, we this day have come to worship you because we love you. We have also come because we all, in one way or another, need to be healed. As we go from this place, may we be constant in prayer so that you might be with us. May the love of God and the peace of Christ be with you always. Amen.*

---

1. *Daily Guideposts* (Mt. Carmel, New York: Guideposts, 1986), p. 303.

2. Howard Clark Kee, *Medicine, Miracle and Magic in New Testament Times* (Cambridge: Cambridge University Press, 1986), pp. 78-79.

3. John Sutherland Bonnell, *Do You Want to be Healed?"* (New York: Harper & Row, 1968), p. 31.

4. George A. Buttrick, *Prayer* (Nashville: Abingdon-Cokesbury Press, 1941), p. 118.

5. Norman Cousins, *Anatomy of an Illness* (New York: Norton, 1979), p. 107.

For Those On The Outside
Luke 8:43-48

Let us pray: O Lord, as I seek to preach the word, and as your people struggle to know who you are, let our minds in these moments be illuminated with understanding from your Holy Spirit. Now may my words be thy words, as I seek to preach the gospel. In Jesus' name we pray, Amen.

The New Testament lesson this morning is about a woman on the periphery; it is the story of one who stood on the outside of the life and ministry of Jesus. She plays only a minor role in the New Testament and preachers do not often choose to preach sermons on this text.

Interpreters of the Bible have not known what to do with this story and it has been regarded by some critics as a miracle tale, full of superstition and magic which does not even belong in the New Testament. The account of this woman follows the more well-known story of Jesus' healing of Jairus' daughter. Therefore, we do not see this woman's name remembered in books and on monuments, and she is not heralded as a great disciple of our Lord. She simply vanishes from the scene almost as quickly as she arrives. She remains anonymous.

Nevertheless, despite her lack of identification, and despite what appears to be her lack of importance, this woman who needs help is not lost in the crowd. The beautiful thing about this story is that even though the encounter between this woman and Jesus takes place in the midst of a dense throng of people, Jesus speaks to the woman as if she were the only person in the world.

We read in the newspaper recently of voices behind a closed chapel door at a shelter for the homeless on the North Side of Pittsburgh, which wailed the words of the old gospel hymn "Do Not Pass Me By," as census takers waited to count the homeless.[1] And yet that is what most of us do. We simply walk on by when we see these poor, dirty and sickly people.

It is a national disgrace that we allow mentally disturbed adults and children of poor families to live on the streets, eating garbage, freezing in bitter cold weather. The newspaper columnist Anthony Lewis condemns the United States as a country which refuses to face its problems. He asks this haunting question: "How many of us, middle-aged or older, ever thought we would walk down an American street as we would Calcutta, indifferent to desperation because we are so hardened to it?"[2]

One of the most important messages of this passage is that Jesus did not just walk on by without stopping. Although almost everyone else in that crowd probably regarded this woman as unimportant, to Jesus she was a human being who was in need. In this moment, Jesus took himself out of the crowd and our Lord gave himself to her as if she were the only one he had to love.

This is the story of a woman who had a flow of blood for 12 years. Her affliction was most likely a continuous uterine hemorrhage, a condition which is both weakening and embarrassing. Like the illness of so many we know personally in our lives, this woman's affliction had left her both poor and discouraged.

We learn from Mark's account that she had "suffered much under many physicians, and had spent all that she had, and was not better, but grew worse (Mark 5:26)." She had exhausted all earthly possibilities for a cure, and had become a broken and depressed human being. She was ready to grab at any solution that could bring her relief from her pain.

This anonymous woman paints a striking picture of a person who came to Jesus as a last resort. She had been led to believe by the talk of the people in the streets that this man Jesus of Nazareth possessed a supernatural power of healing. This is the reason why this woman sought Jesus out in the first place.

Obviously, we would say that this woman came to Jesus for the wrong reasons. She did not come seeking Jesus because she wanted to hear his message, nor did she come because she wanted to establish a personal relationship with this Son of God. This woman did not plan to stand before Jesus face to face and ask forgiveness for her sins.

No, this woman wanted only to touch the robe of Jesus, so that the healing power of the Lord God would cure her of this cursed physical affliction.

Are not so many of us like this woman? We exhaust all of our worldly possibilities before we come to God, the true God for help. This woman is simply one example of those individuals who seek healing and happiness in things other than the Spirit of God. Is it not true, that for many of us and those we know, medicine has replaced faith as a source of healing power? We trust physicians more than we trust our God, and yet inevitably there comes a time when doctors are unable to perform the miracles that seem implicitly promised in high-tech machinery and medications.[3] It is not unusual for persons to become angry at God, even though they have trusted others first and only, and have not been helped.

For others of us, we may not seek physical healing, but rather we search for happiness in things other than the fruits of the spirit. In other areas of life, we exhaust all of our earthly possibilities before we come to God seeking happiness. We may seek fulfillment in a higher paying job, or a more prestigious position. For others it may be obtaining the right degree from the right college. For a nation it may be gaining military superiority. We may hold the vain hope that changing politicians will solve all of our problems.

It may be any number of things, but we seem to be people who are constantly seeking security in things other than God. Like this woman, we are often reluctant to seek Christ except as a last resort. Why is it that we cannot really believe the biblical truth that "there is no other name under heaven . . . by which we must be saved (Acts 4:12)?"

So like this woman, we fail to make our commitment to Jesus Christ. We instead prefer to stay in the background, where we are safe. We stay there often because to seek Christ first requires a commitment which we feel that we are not able to make, or simply do not want to make, because our energies are channeled in so many other directions. Like this woman, we remain anonymous and on the periphery of the life of the church. This is a natural human tendency to which most of us are subject at one time or another in our lives.

When we do finally come to seek this Jesus of Nazareth, it may be for the wrong reasons, as it was for this woman. We may enter a particular church because of its prestige, or another church because it offers simple answers to complex and difficult questions. We may come to this holy place only because we want to be among our friends.

The woman in this story came seeking Jesus with the hope that his magic power would heal her disease. One would think that before Jesus could deal with this woman that he would correct her wild and crazy notions. He should have told her that this business about magical healing was nonsense. We might think that he should have told her that it was his message about the love of God and the love of humanity that was his true purpose for being on earth. Like the minister who reprimands his congregation for coming to church only on Christmas or Easter, Jesus could have asked this woman: "Why are you here now? Don't you have a good reason for coming to see me?"

But Jesus did nothing of the sort, because Jesus knew that God's love is extended to all people, and that no one is rejected if they come to him. It was for this reason that this woman was not lost in the crowd. For you see, Jesus doesn't set conditions, or ask a person to fulfill certain eligibility requirements. He instead asks us to come to him just as we are — and we need only to touch his garment and he will embrace us, just as a mother will embrace a child who has been mischievous.

I am certain that there are many people who have entered the door of the church, not really knowing why they have come.

Perhaps they have come here because they are lonely. Perhaps there are young men and women who enter the ministry who are not certain of what they are doing.

But God works in mysterious ways. God can take persons who are unsure or confused about their motivations and transform them. God can reach into people's hearts and nurture faint callings until they become strong callings. We need only first to seek this Jesus, to give him an opening and let his light shine in. This is often all that is needed in order for us to be healed.

There is a story about an American sculptor who was served by a maid with a bad temper. She clearly did not understand what the sculptor did for a living, or even what this man did with his time. Every time the maid came into his studio, she pushed her broom, looking at the floor, grumbling about how sloppy a craftsman this man was.

This maid never paid any attention to the beautiful sculptures this man created, and she never recognized the skill that he exercised as he created these carefully crafted works of art.

One day the maid announced that she would be taking a month's vacation. The sculptor was very happy to be relieved of her nasty temper and oppressive personality. As she went away on her vacation, the artist dedicated himself with unlimited energy to a particular sculpture, now that he was free of all interruptions.

When the maid returned, she threw open the door and was startled. She stared at the statue he had completed and then exclaimed: "It's Abraham Lincoln!" For the first time in his life, the sculptor felt some affection for this cleaning woman. He replied, "Yes, indeed, it is Abraham Lincoln." But then the woman's eyes narrowed, she glared at the sculptur and said, "How did you know that he was in there?"

Sometimes, when life seems very difficult, dark and empty, sometimes we fear that our Lord God will not see us in our granite, we feel that we are lost in the crowd. We are afraid that we will be left as half-finished, unfulfilled and unnoticed people, people who can never be made whole or happy.

But God does know who is inside that block of granite. Our true self, our real caring self may be hidden by the many walls we set up around us. Those may be walls of anger or jealousy. If we have an illness, we may have allowed that illness to control us, to dominate us to the point where we cannot function as loving, caring human beings. In some way, we isolate ourselves from God and other people.

However, if we can admit to ourselves that we are not complete, that we are not all self-sufficient, if we can open ourselves up just a little — then God can find our true soul which is buried in stone. If we seek Christ in even a small way, then we will feel the chisel and mallet of the Lord God beginning to set us free, so that we may be healed of our afflictions and thus made whole and happy and free.

This anonymous woman came to Jesus seeking a magical cure, but she came away understanding the mystery of faith, the real depth of faith. Jesus healed her through his attention and his love. Because in the end she did trust him to heal her. Jesus was able to say to her: "Daughter your faith has made you well."

We are people who always have put our trust in other people and other things in our search for wholeness, health and happiness. But in the end, only faith will heal us.

Let our prayer this day be that we may place our trust in the Lord, so that we may come to trust the power and grace of God that can make us whole, and happy and free.

Benediction: Father, your name and your nature are love. Grant to us this day the courage to serve you with all that is in us, all that we may ever be. Now may the peace of Christ, which passes all our understanding, keep your hearts and minds in the knowledge of God, and of his son Jesus Christ. The blessing of God the Father, the Son and the Holy

Spirit be among you, and remain with you always. Amen.

---

1. *Pittsburgh Post Gazette,* March 21, 1990, p. 1.

2. Anthony Lewis, "One Country Still Refuses to Face Its Problems." *Pittsburgh Post Gazette,* February 21, 1990, p. 7.

3. Douglas Shenson, "Limits of the Possible," *New York Times Magazine,* May 29, 1988, p. 30.

Who Is This?
Matthew 21:1-11

> *Let us pray: Gracious and eternal God, we come to you this day seeking to have your Holy Spirit lead us as we enter the week which is called "holy." May we in these moments deepen our faith and draw closer to Jesus as we reflect upon what he has done for us. In his precious name we pray. Amen.*

We have sung together "Were You There When They Crucified My Lord?" The words of this old and familiar hymn give us reason to pause and consider the meaning of Christ's sacrifice for us as he gave his all so that we may be freed from the sin and guilt that plague our lives and keep us from being all that we can be.

But the truth of the matter is that no, we were not there when they crucified our Lord. We were not there to witness people lining the streets, waving palms, laying down their coats for Jesus to walk upon. They cried out "Hosanna, Hosanna," which means "save now." "Blessed is he who comes in the name of the Lord."

Even though we come to church and receive palms; even though we hear the Scripture which tells us what happened in those days , and even though we pray to a living Lord, we were not there.

Nevertheless, even though we were not on the street for that first Palm Sunday parade, we are in one particular way very much like some of the people in that crowd. Although we profess to know and to follow this Jesus of Nazareth, like those people in the crowd, we, too, ask the question: "Who is this? Who is this, really?"

Some believed that Jesus should have been an armed messiah, a military leader. These people believed that they could be free only if they were to throw off the yoke of Roman oppression. In every war, there have been people who have believed that military victory would bring a lasting peace and prosperity that would free them from all of their troubles. However, that kind of victory has always brought disappointment. Just look at what is happening in places which have recently experienced revolution — Eastern Europe, Nicaragua, the Philippines. The struggle, the pain, the suffering continues even in the midst of newfound freedom.

Then there were those in that Palm Sunday crowd who believed that Jesus was an imposter, a troublemaker. Indeed, Jesus did upset the religious establishment. He healed on the Sabbath, which angered those whose narrow religion seemed to have lost any compassion for the sick and the weak.

Furthermore, in the passage following the Palm Sunday account, we read how Jesus entered the temple and drove out the money-changers and those who were selling in the temple of God. Jesus angered the priests and elders by telling them that they had made his Father's house of prayer into a den of robbers.

Who is this man Jesus? That is the question that all those who call themselves Christians must ask this week. Who is this man Jesus, and what does he mean for our lives?

We are mistaken if we believe that this Jesus came to free us from all of our earthly cares or suffering. Many people we know seek and want that kind of Jesus. As we have been finding in our consideration of the healing ministry of Jesus, our Lord did do miraculous things as he healed those who were blind, lame, deaf, afflicted with leprosy. Jesus made it very clear to us that God intends that we live our lives as whole, healthy and happy persons.

Yet despite the fact that Jesus did everything that he could to alleviate the pain and suffering for other people, he could not escape suffering himself. Yes, when he entered Jerusalem on Palm Sunday he was heralded as a king. However, it would not be very long before he was betrayed, not only by Judas, but by all of the other disciples as they denied their allegiance to their Lord. As you will recall, only the women would remain faithful to him.

We see then that Jesus had to confront the reality of evil head-on before he could defeat it. He had to be spat upon, beaten, crucified as a common criminal before he could overcome evil. The glory of the gospel lies in the fact that Jesus did all of this suffering for us. As Jesus became one of us, he came to know our pain because he himself suffered. Through the life of Jesus, we have learned that suffering and evil are just part of human existence that not even our Lord could escape.

So when we ask ourselves, "Who is this Jesus?", we need to acknowledge first of all that he is the one who suffered and died for us so that we might be freed from sin. However, we need also to understand that Jesus is the one who suffers with us, the one who feels our pain whenever we suffer. This is one way that Jesus brings healing power into our lives. For those who suffer, this may be the most obvious way that God in Christ can become a part of our lives.

No, we were not there when Jesus suffered and died. But he is surely there with us and for us when we suffer rejection and physical pain. Dorothee Soelle makes this important point about suffering and salvation: "Redemption does not come to people from outside or from above. God wants to use people in order to work on the completion of his creation. Precisely for this reason God must also suffer with the creation."[1]

I recently picked up a volume in a used book store by the Swedish author Par Lagerkvist titled *Barabbas*. This is a fictional novel about the noted criminal who was released by Pilate as an act of mercy when Jesus was arraigned before he was put to death on a cross. You will recall that given the choice between releasing Barabbas and Jesus, the crowd shouted "free Barabbas," even though he was a robber, murderer and revolutionary. This, of course, happened only a few short days after these same people had shouted praises to Jesus on Palm Sunday as he entered the city of Jerusalem, heralded as their new king. According to the novel, this Barabbas had personally witnessed Jesus' crucifixion.

The novel about Barabbas tells how this fortunate criminal became a Roman slave and was transported to the island of Cyprus, where he went to work in the copper mines. There he is assigned to work side by side with an old Armenian slave named Sahak, who is a faithful follower of Jesus Christ.

All Roman slaves were required to wear a metal disk on a chain around their necks which bore the mark of the Roman State, signifying that they were the property of Caesar. However, Sahak had scratched some strange markings on the back of his disk which spelled out the name "Christos Iesus," which means Jesus Christ in Greek. This was his way of testifying that his primary loyalty was to Jesus Christ, even though he was offically owned by the Roman Emperor.

Impressed with the faith of his new friend, Barabbas tells the old Christian that he, too, would like to be a disciple of this Jesus. The two slaves then work together and scratch the words "Jesus Christ" in Greek on the disk of Barabbas.

However, one of the foremen overheard what was going on, and this information is reported to the governor of the island. Both Sahak and Barabbas are brought before him and are questioned about the markings on their disks.

The Christian Sahak tells the governor that this Jesus is the name of his God, who is also the God of everyone. Sahak says, "I belong to him." The governor reminds him that he belongs to the State. In pledging allegiance to this Jesus, the governor explains that Sahak was setting himself against Caesar, who is also a god. He warns the slave that having other gods before Caesar was a crime punishable by death.

The governor then turns to Barabbas. He says, "Do you also believe in this god whose name is on your disk? Barabbas shakes his head no. "Is he not your god? Isn't that what this inscription means?" asks the governor. Barabbas answers softly, "I have no god."

After several moments of silence, the governor then asks old Sahak the Christian the same questions. "Do you grasp the full implications of what you have said? If you renounce your faith no harm shall come to you . . . Will you do it?"

Sahak responds, "I cannot." "Why not?" the governor asks. Sahak replies. "I cannot deny my God." "Extraordinary man," the governor says as he orders Sahak to be taken away and crucified for his witness to his Lord.

Then the governor takes his dagger, and grasping the disk of Barabbas in one hand, he scratches its point across the words "Christos Iesus." He says, "There's really no need, as you don't believe in him in any case . . . ." He then commends the slave for his sensible behavior, and orders that he be rewarded. Barabbas then wears the disk with the crossed out name of Jesus for the rest of his life.[2]

Is not this the problem with the Christianity that we witness in the lives of so many people both in and outside of our churches? We want to carry the name of Jesus as long as it is fun, as long as it is easy, as long as it is the popular and sensible thing to do. We will profess the name of Jesus when we need a healing, or whenever we are in the midst of a crisis situation. Indeed, as the gospel writer John says in his account of the Palm Sunday parade, it sometimes appears as if "the whole world has gone after" Jesus (John 12:19). It especially seems that way to us at Christmas or Easter time.

But how many are really ready to stand by Jesus and his church when we are asked to give something up for him? We ask the world of God, but then what are we really giving back to him day in and day out?

For so many people, it is so easy just to cross the name of Jesus from our lives, and then simply live without him. In this day and age, when life is so comfortable and prosperous for so many people, men and women can do just that, because like Barabbas, in their heart of hearts, they do not really believe in the saving power of this Jesus. But if we do not believe, our lives cannot be whole. One tragedy for those who do not have faith is that when healing is needed for body, mind or human relationship, they do not know how to open themselves to the healing power of the Master.

As your pastor, on this Palm Sunday, I must ask you: who is Jesus for you this day? Are you seeking Christ's healing power for yourself and for others? Is he truly Lord and Master of your life? Do you really make prayer and commitment to the church of Jesus Christ the number one priority in your life? Or would it really matter to you if the name of Jesus was crossed from your existence forever?

My friends in Christ, Holy Week provides us with the opportunity to focus oureselves anew upon a life of discipleship — to take seriously once again Jesus Christ and his church — to realize the difference that Christ can make in our lives. It is time to rededicate our lives to the One who has lived and died so that we might be freed from the sins of the past and then live in peace and happiness for all eternity.

> *Benediction: Our Lord and our God, we have sung hosanna to thy name, and we have experienced the presence of Christ in our lives. As we go from this place, we remember that in this week Christ will die, but that he will live again. That after we go through the dark night of Good Friday, we will celebrate again your glory come Easter morning, as Christ is risen. Now may the love of God, the peace of Christ and the fellowship of the Holy Spirit be with you always, Amen.*

---

1. Dorothee Soelle, *Suffering,* trans. Everett Kalin (Philadelphia: Fortress Press, 1975), p. 146.

2. Par Lagerkvist, *Barabbas,* trans. Alan Blair (New York: Bantam Books, 1972), pp. 117-122.

A Joyful New Beginning
John 20:1-18

> *Let us pray: Gracious and everliving Father, on this day which is greater than all the days, we come seeking to understand the eternal message of the gospel and how it may transform our lives. May we in these moments not only come to know that Jesus lives, but may we come to know him as brother and friend. In Christ's holy name we pray, Amen.*

The philosopher Sidney Hook writes in an article titled "In Defense of Voluntary Euthanasia" about how at one point in his life he was near death. The treatment for his congestive heart failure had triggered a stroke. His left side and vocal cords became paralyzed and pleurisy set into his body. He lay for weeks in pain and misery connected to life-support machines in the hospital. At one point his heart stopped beating altogether, but just as he lost consciousness, his heart was thumped back into action once again by the doctors.

At another time when he was relatively clear-headed, Mr. Hook asked his physician to discontinue life-support services, or to show him how to do it himself, so as to relieve the doctor of any moral responsibility. However, the doctor refused. He said that someday Mr. Hook would appreciate how unwise that request made in a state of pain and suffering really was.

One month later Professor Hook was discharged from the hospital, and in six months' time he had regained the use of his arms and legs and voice. He went back to work as a writer and philosopher, for he still had contributions to make. As he reflects upon this apparent healing, Mr. Hook comments that some people might see his experience as an argument against allowing the requests of patients who want to die to be honored.

But Sidney Hook says that he does not. Having lived a full and happy life, he does not wish to suffer another heart attack, or to burden his wife and children any longer with his infirmity. In his maturity of 80 plus years, he has realized that death is not the worst thing that can happen. He quotes the ancient sage Seneca, who observed long ago that "the wise man will live as long as he ought, not as long as he can."[1]

I share this story with you because it helps us to appreciate one of the great themes of the resurrection story and the entire Easter event, which is that death is not the final word in life. In the story of Christ's rising from the dead we receive a hope that can sustain us and uphold us no matter what happens to us, no matter how difficult our circumstances become in life. People who have lived their lives in faith and are at peace with God and themselves have no need to stand in fear of death.

Easter Day is that time when you and I gather together in this church among our families and friends to reflect upon what God has done for us. We come together to worship in wonder and amazement at the resurrection of God's son who is Christ our Lord. This is also a time to reflect upon the resurrection of the human race — God's message to us that indeed we can be forgiven for our sins and freed to live in love and peace for all of eternity.

So let us then consider the two vital messages of the day — the power of immortality and the power of the risen and present Christ.

The resurrection of Jesus from the dead affirms what the New Testament records speak of as "eternal life," the conviction which Christians hold that our souls are truly immortal and will live forever. When you and I witness immortality in the man Jesus Christ, our lives take on a new and different meaning. We can think of our lives in a different context, for we know that what is here and now is not all there is.

The Roman Emperor Vespasian once said, "I will die on my feet, as becomes an Emperor." For the word emperor, we can substitute the words "man" or "woman." It certainly becomes a man or woman to go on with life with as much intensity as one can to the end of one's days, especially if that person claims to be a disciple of Jesus Christ.[2] But as we travel the rough and rocky roads of life, it is sometimes very difficult to remember that fact. No man or woman here today needs to be lectured on the frail and precarious nature of life on earth. Illness or accident can cut down any one of us at any time. How easily our dreams can be foiled or damaged by our mistakes or by the behind-the-scenes workings of people who are jealous or just do not like us. How fragile are those great dreams of one's youth which are so often trampled upon by a cruel and careless world.

Paul's words written to the Philippians can be very helpful to us as we face obstacles and setbacks in living. As he sat in his prison cell and wrote these words, the apostle must have been very disappointed with the way in which his ministry of 15 years was turning out. He had been let down by fellow workers such as Demas and even Peter. Nobody had supported him at his first trial. The church in Corinth was constantly fighting and bickering over stupid issues. All of these disappointments could have resulted in bitterness and resignation for a person of weaker faith.

Yet in the midst of his personal struggle, Paul was able to write these words: "Brethren, I do not consider that I have made it my own; but one thing I do, forgetting what lies behind and straining forward to what lies ahead, I press on toward the goal for the prize of the upward call of God in Jesus Christ (Philippians 2:13-14)." When people see themselves as immortal and conceive of life as eternal, then they, like Paul, will never view death and defeat as the final chapter in human existence.

Our faith then enables us to see disappointments and defeats as simply the conditions of our discipleship. They are the terms on which we must live the life that God has granted to us. Therefore, we need not let the shattering of dreams, or even the onset of age and illness disillusion us or leave us in despair. For although we know that this life is on the whole very good indeed, we realize that this life is only a foretaste, perhaps even a training ground for the life to come. The purpose of living is different when we witness and accept our essential human nature as being eternal and immortal.

It is true that a glance at the morning newspaper can be very saddening. This daily ritual does not cause us to have much faith in men and women. Leaders of great and well-educated nations cannot begin to agree on how to eliminate the terrible thermonuclear weapons that we point at each other in fear and ignorance. Thousands of lives are threatened because we cannot adequately control the hazardous chemicals that pass through our neighborhoods on trucks and trains. Men, women and children of all ages are killed every day because we will not deal firmly and responsibly with those weak people who drive under the influence of drugs and alcohol. It does appear at times that the evil in the world is getting the better of the human race.

However, the fact that our nature is immortal and that God is with us at all times means that we can face the troubles of the world head-on. We can meet these problems and defeat them, because we need not be afraid to take risks. We need not be fearful, because God will be with us no matter what we do if we follow the way of Christ.

When we make God part of our lives and accept the gift of immortality, then we are freed to make real investments in other people. You all know how difficult those investments can be, for we may not see any immediate payoffs. Sacrifice in a marriage can be incredibly difficult at times. Investing time with children may appear to be a waste of time if those children reject their parents and seem to care only about themselves. Taking care of elderly and sick relatives may seem to be a useless drain of time and money, leading to resentment. The energy expended in working with the mentally or physically handicapped may seem to be of little value, for the work can be so terribly frustrating.

But only God who is the Lord of time and history can really know what will happen in the long run to an investment in people. We may not be able to see any results, even any miraculous healings, in our own lifetime, but as we grow in age and maturity, we will come to know that many of those people we have known and loved have been gathered into a life eternal. For example, a man or woman of faith who has lost a spouse often just knows in his or her heart that the husband or wife lives on in eternity.

This is what the great Episcopal preacher Phillips Brooks has called the "echo of the Resurrection of Christ." This is when we come to feel in our spirits and in our hearts the very presence of those who have moved into a life beyond our immediate vision. We come to discover that our investments in those around us are never lost as we move from this earthly life into life with God in heaven. For we are bound together with those we love in God's mighty act of salvation which has been made real in the resurrection of Jesus Christ in the community of saints. There really is all the reason in the world for us to care about people both now and in the future. Resurrection is then the foundation for the healing ministry of the church.

However, the message that life for us is eternal and that we will live forever is really only an aside to this great Easter story. Easter is not a "happily ever after" ending to God's story in Jesus Christ. The risen Lord himself calls us to live in his joy now and forever. That is what it means to participate in the joy of eternal life. Easter Day presents us with an opportunity for a joyful new beginning which can enable us to make sense out of our past and to hope for the future.

The greater message is that we can experience the power of the risen Christ here and now. This is the reason why we are here dressed in our newest and best clothing this glorious Easter Day. Because Christ lives, we can be forgiven, healed and transformed into new people.

There is a beautiful valley in Switzerland which is deeply hidden in that mountain range known as the Alps. That valley is completely surrounded by steep mountain walls. If one enters this valley, that person will move along the only road until it ends at the base of a steep wall of rock.

The Swiss call this place the "End of the World." However, if one is willing to go climbing by foot, Swiss guides will show a determined hiker the path that leads up and over that mountain barrier.

Reflecting upon this natural phenomenon, Harleigh Rosenberger comments that many people believe that life is like a road that runs through the valley of time. "We cannot turn back but must continue walking onward. The days pass quickly and then comes the end of the road. We stand at the sheer rock wall we call death. It is the end of our world, for it is the end of life."[3]

Because Jesus Christ has been raised from the dead and we have through him received the gift of eternal life, we find a way up and over that wall of rock. Jesus said, "I am the resurrection and the life; he who believes in me, though he die, yet shall he live, and whoever lives and believes in me shall never die (John 11:25)."

My friends in Christ, our hope is grounded in the gift of eternal life which we receive this day — it is our way out of the valley of darkness and despair through which all of us walk at one time or another in our lives. This gift of eternal life does not begin at death. It begins now for all who worship the risen Christ. This life eternal will then continue beyond the grave into the life to come, for our souls are eternal, and in Christ we become one with the Father who made us. This is the hope and the promise which we receive this glorious Easter Day.

As we go from this place of worship, I challenge you to celebrate the resurrection every week and every day of your life. Be glad in your heart that Jesus Christ is raised from the dead and that you will live forever if you can only believe and follow. Let us today make a joyful new beginning in Jesus Christ.

Benediction: Gracious and eternal Father, on this Easter day we have sung Hallelujah, Hallelujah — yes, we have sung praises to thy name, for Jesus

Christ is risen, and he lives in our hearts. Help us then in the weeks and months ahead not to forget the reason why we are here. Lord, may Christ's rising from the dead enable us to become disciples again. Amen.

---

1. Sidney Hook, "In Defense of Voluntary Euthanasia," *New York Times,* 1 March 1987, sec. 4, p. 25.

2. Dom Hubert van Zeller, *We Die Standing Up* (Garden City, New York: Image Books, 1961), p. 30.

3. Harleigh M. Rosenberger, *Thoughts Along the Road* (Valley Forge: Judson Press, 1966), p. 119.

Beginning A Healing Ministry

In this chapter I would like to share briefly the reasons why I decided to initiate a healing ministry in my parish, and some of the steps that a pastor might take in initiating public healing services in his or her local church.

As pastor of a predominantly older congregation, I became increasingly concerned about the many members who were experiencing physical difficulties, many of which were related to advancing age. Furthermore, I was perplexed by the suffering, frustration and depression that accompany illness and injury in younger men and women. Having experienced an unfortunate division of the congregation over a proposed building program, I was also grieved over the many broken relationships that occurred within the faith community. These concerns prompted me to begin reading about the healing ministry of the church, and I attended the conference on healing and wholeness which is held annually at the Port Vue United Methodist Church, McKeesport, Pennsylvania.

I became convinced that this is an area of ministry to which our churches have not been giving sufficient attention. The reasons for this are usually based upon a misunderstanding of the purpose and methods of the traditional healing ministry of the Christian church. The most prevalent reservation about instituting public healing services is that they will be associated with the sensational work of faith healers, some of whom have made a charade of the healing ministry, sometimes on nationwide television. There are faith healers who discourage sick people from seeking medical assistance, which often results in personal tragedy. It is important to understand right from the beginning that the traditional and legitimate healing ministry of the Christian church must be disassociated from the work of these faith healers.

Dietrich Bonhoeffer wrote: "Love toward sick members should have a special place in the Christian congregation. Christ comes near to us in the sick."[1] It is often when we are most vulnerable that God's power and love can become real to us, and we are seldom more vulnerable than when we are seriously ill. The church that is present to provide the means of grace to sick people is one that is responding to the call of Jesus to minister to those who are in need. We need to remember that sickness and healing are not merely individual concerns, but the responsibility of the whole body of Christ.

Before beginning a healing ministry, it is of critical importance that the pastor be very clear about the purpose and design of this worship experience. The reason for this is, as mentioned, that the healing ministry is so often misunderstood. The minister should do extensive reading in this area, and if possible, attend a seminar on healing ministries so that he is knowledgeable about the scriptural and traditional basis for this ministry. This will enable him to field potential criticism effectively.[2]

The pastor should then enter into dialogue with lay leadership in order to generate support and enthusiasm. A study on healing may be offered in the Sunday school classes or other settings. One excellent resource for such a study is James Wagner's *Blessed to Be a Blessing*. A series of Sunday sermons on the healing ministry of Jesus will promote an understanding of this ministry throughout the congregation. It is advisable to receive approval from the church's administrative council.

The most important task of the church's healing ministry is to pray for those who are ill and those who are experiencing broken relationships. How many times have we heard individuals say that in the process of healing, they "could feel" the prayers of others?

Certainly we cannot appeal to medical science to confirm the truth of our faith. However, both the Bible and modern testimonies confirm that when prayers are uttered on behalf of one who is sick, "something" happens, and that there are indeed "results" of one sort or another. William Temple is said to have remarked that when he prayed for people "coincidences" happened, and that when he stopped praying, the "coincidences" stopped happening.[3]

It is true that some people do not receive the particular healing for which they and their loved ones have prayed. However, in every instance, healing of one sort or another does happen. There is no such thing as unanswered prayer. In one way or another, the healing ministry enables people to experience the power of God's spirit in their lives. Often God's response to prayer is the gift of strength, with which a person is enabled to cope with a serious illness or disability.

There are a number of ways in which a new emphasis on prayer can be incorporated into the healing ministry as well as the total life of the parish. At our church, we utilize a prayer journal in which members write the names of those friends and loved ones who are in need of prayers for physical and relational healing prior to the Sunday morning service. These names are shared with the congregation during the worship hour during a "Prayer and Praise Time." During the week, I, as pastor, pray individually for these persons. These names are then lifted up to God at our monthly services of prayer and healing. Some churches use prayer cards which are placed in the pews and then brought forward for prayer at an appropriate time during the service.

The three vital components of the public healing service are the sacrament of holy communion, the anointing with oil, and the laying-on of hands. The purpose of sharing the eucharist is that this worship experience focuses our attention on Jesus Christ who is the Great Physician. It is the opportunity to confess our sin and then receive God's gift of forgiveness. We do not come to these services primarily to see our friends or to hear the sermon. We instead concentrate on opening our hearts and minds to the Spirit embodied in the living Christ who becomes present in the sharing of the bread and the cup.

Why does the pastor anoint the people with oil? In biblical times olive oil was considered to be the best medicine of the age. We remember how the Good Samaritan anointed with oil the wounds of the man who had been beaten, and how the apostles "anointed with oil many who were sick and healed them (Mark 6:13)." In the healing service, people are anointed so that they may fully experience the power of prayer united with medicine. We receive this instruction from James in the New Testament: "Is any among you sick? Let him call the elders of the church, and let us pray over him, anointing him with oil in the name of the Lord . . . (James 5:14)."

In the healing service, the pastor can use the oil to make the sign of the cross on the parishioner, using the words, "I anoint you in the name of the Father, Son and Holy Spirit." It is recommended that olive oil mixed with frankincense and myrrh be used, because this mixture does not spoil, as does pure olive oil.[4]

The laying-on-of-hands was practiced by Jesus as he transmitted God's healing power to those who were sick or disabled. Today, it is a tangible expression of Christ operating in and through us as we minister in his name. This practice is simply another channel of God's love and healing power. The minister simply lays his right hand on the head of the parishioner and offers a personal prayer for healing.

How often should these services be held? Some churches have found the enthusiasm to be so great that the services are held weekly. Such regularity speaks of the great value which the people ascribe to this ministry. Indeed, there are almost always sick people among us, people who stand in need of prayer and healing.

My personal experience has been that the monthly service has been the most appropriate for our parish and fits well into a busy church calendar at all times during the year. As with all new and exciting ministries, one must be careful not to overextend oneself, because of the dangers of burnout and overexposure. If the monthly services are being enthusiastically received, then the church might consider having them more frequently.

The positive response to public services of prayer and healing at many parishes throughout the world has demonstrated that this ministry can be an important part of the church's mission to both its members and the community. I would encourage all churches to consider instituting this ministry which seeks to share God's healing power. It can be another significant source of revitalization for the faith community.

---

1. Bonhoeffer quoted by F. Burton Nelson, "What Churches Can Do," *Christianity Today,* September 10, 1990, p. 36.

2. The United Methodist Church sponsors "Adventures in Healing and Wholeness," a program designed as an introduction to the healing ministry of the church. Contact Dr. James Wagner, Director, Prayer and Healing Ministries, The Upper Room, P.O. Box 189, Nashville, Tennessee 37202-0189. A Conference on Healing and Wholeness is held annually at the Port Vue United Methodist Church, 1565 Washington Boulevard, McKeesport, Pennsylvania 15133. Rev. Donald Bartow also sponsors conferences on healing. Write to The Spiritial Healing Ministry, P.O. Box 92, Canton, Ohio 44708.

3. Michael J. Paton and W. Lawton Tonge, "Prayer and Healing," *Religion and Medicine 3*, ed. D. W. Millard (London: SCM Press, LTD, 1976), pp. 21-22.

4. This oil may be obtained from New Hope Anointing Oil, St. Simons Isle, Georgia 31522.

A Worship Service

Of Holy Communion, Prayer And Healing

"Be still and know that I am God (Psalm 46:10)."

Prelude: A time for personal prayer and meditation

Christian Greetings: Pastor

*Call to Worship

> Leader: We come as a people of God seeking healing and wholeness for our bodies, our minds and our spirits.
>
> **People: God knows all our pain and unhappiness; God's love will save us from suffering and death.**
>
> Leader: We can place our total trust in God; God's presence is always with us.
>
> **People: Let us now praise God for Christ's healing power which gives us the strength to live.**

Hymn

Prayer of Confession *(In unison)*

Almighty and everliving God, we confess that we are men and women who have not always trusted in your desire and ability to heal us of all our afflictions. We have not always come to you first in prayer when we experience illness and distress. We admit that we have not taken good care of your gifts to us of our bodies, our minds and our relationships. We confess that we have not always been steadfast in our search for peace.

Forgive us, Lord, for these our sins of commission and omission. Have mercy upon us in this hour of prayer. Through Jesus Christ we pray, Amen.

Moments of Personal Confession (in silence)

Assurance of Pardon

> Leader: If we confess our sins, God who is faithful and just will forgive our sins. God's infinite love will cleanse us of all that is not right in our hearts.

People: Thanks be to God.

The Peace

> Leader: The peace of Christ be with you.

People: And with your spirit.

The pastor and people may greet one another in the name of Christ.

Scripture Lesson

Meditation

*Hymn

Prayers of the People

> Leader: It has been said that "prayer is the work of the church."[1] Let us then be in an attitude of prayer as the names of those who stand in need of healing are shared.

Unison Prayer of Petition and Intercession

O God who made yourself known to us in the miracle of your Son Jesus, you are the source of all peace and healing in the world. We offer unto you now our prayers for those persons whose names have been shared this evening. These and many others stand in need of spiritual, physical and relational healing this day.

May your healing power and presence come upon all those who are in pain and suffering so that they may be made whole once again; may they know that you are an ever present help in time of trouble. Through Jesus Christ, who is the Great Physician, we pray, Amen.

The Sacrament of Holy Communion

The Invitation

Leader: All who are present are invited to the table of the Lord. We ask only that you come with a love for Jesus and a desire to live in peace with others.

The Prayer of Consecration: Pastor

Gracious and eternal God, we thank you for sending your only Son into the world to be our holy Savior. Your Spirit came upon Jesus and appointed him to preach good news to the poor to proclaim release to the captives, and enable those who were blind to recover their sight. Jesus healed the sick, ate with sinners and fed the hungry. Through his baptism, death and resurrection, he saved us from suffering and death.

On the night in which he gave himself up for us, Jesus took bread, gave thanks to you, broke the bread, gave it to his disciples and said: "Take, eat; this is my body which is given for you. Do this in remembrance of me."

When the supper was over, Jesus took the cup, gave thanks to you, gave it to the disciples and said: "Drink from this, all of you; for this is my blood of the new covenant which is poured out for you and for many for the forgiveness of sins. Do this, as often as you drink it, in remembrance of me."

The Communion of the People

The Prayer of Thanksgiving (in unison)

God of love and glory, we thank you for this opportunity to experience the mystery of healing, wholeness and new life which has come to us in this holy sacrament. May we as the body of Christ share with others the grace and peace which you have granted us in these moments. In his name we pray, Amen.

Hymn

Prayers for Personal Healing

You are invited to come to the chancel rail to receive anointing with oil and laying-on-of hands as we pray together for you and your loved ones.

A Time of Giving Thanks for our Healings and Other Celebrations

Benediction

Leader: Let us now go out into the world to love and to serve in the name of Jesus Christ.

People: Thanks be to God.

*Congregation standing

---

1. Donald Bartow, *A Ministry of Prayer* (Canton, Ohio: Life Enrichment Publishers [n.d.]), back cover.

Suggested Hymns

For Services Of Prayer And Healing

"Heal Me, Hands of Jesus"

"When Jesus the Healer Passed Through Galilee"

"Jesus' Hands Were Kind Hands"

"There Is a Balm in Gilead"

"Blessed Jesus, at Thy Word"

"Spirit of the Living God"

"Open My Eyes"

"He Touched Me"

"Jesus Is Lord"

"I Need Thee Every Hour"

"Sweet Hour of Prayer"

"He Hideth My Soul"

"Wonderful Peace"

Prepared by Miss Janet Gessner, Music Director, Christy Park United Methodist Church.

Selected Bibliography

Resources For Beginning A Healing Ministry

Althouse, Lawrence W., *Rediscovering the Gift of Healing,* Nashville, Abingdon Press, 1977.

Bartow, Donald W., and King, Blair B., *Beginning the Ministry of Healing,* Canton Ohio: Life Enrichment Publishers, 1974.

Bartow, Donald W., *A Ministry Of Prayer,* 3rd ed. Canton Ohio: Life Enrichment Publisher, 1986.

Bartow, Donald W., *The Adventures of Healing,* Revised ed., Canton, Ohio: Life Enrichment Publishers, 1985.

Kelsey, Morton, *Psychology, Medicine and Christian Healing,* San Francisco: Harper & Row, 1988.

Linn, Dennis, Linn, Matthew, and Fabricant, *Praying With Another for Healing,* Ramsey, New Jersey: Paulist Press, 1984.

McNutt, Francis, *Healing,* Notre Dame: Ave Maria Press, 1974.

McNutt, Francis, *The Power to Heal,* Notre Dame: Ave Maria Press, 1977.

Sanford, John A., *Healing and Wholeness,* Ramsey, New Jersey: Paulist Press, 1977.

Wagner, James K., *Blessed to Be a Blessing,* Nashville: The Upper Room, 1980.

www.ingramcontent.com/pod-product-compliance
Lightning Source LLC
Chambersburg PA
CBHW060853050426
42453CB00008B/962